Pam Harlow

Sunset in a Spider Web

Sijo Poetry of Ancient Korea

Adapted by Virginia Olsen Baron
from translations by Chung Seuk Park

Illustrated by Minja Park Kim

Holt, Rinehart and Winston
New York   Chicago   San Francisco

Sunset in a Spider Web

Library of Congress Cataloging in Publication Data
Baron, Virginia Olsen.
  Sunset in a spider web.
  SUMMARY: A collection of Sijo, one of the earliest
forms of Korean poetry and still the most popular
today.
  1. Sijo—Translations into English. 2. English
poetry—Translations from Korean. [1. Sijo.
2. Korean poetry] I. Park, Chung Seuk, tr.
II. Kim, Minja Park, illus. III. Title.
PL984.E3B3   895.7'1'208   73-14657
ISBN 0-03-012071-3

Published simultaneously in Canada by Holt, Rinehart
and Winston of Canada, Limited.

Printed in the United States of America

First Edition

Introduction

Once someone said that translating poetry from one language to another is like unhooking a spider web from the place where it was spun and hanging it up in a new place. If we were to continue the simile, we could imagine what might happen. The delicate silky strands would get twisted, fused, some spokes might break off and be lost. The fragile beauty is bound to be diminished once the web is separated from its original home. What then is the use of even trying?

In transplanting both the poetry and the spider's web, the chances are that whatever peripheral damage is done, the center will still hold. The spider can mend his web and the translator can substitute other words in other languages to try to achieve effects similar to those of the original poem. The result is never perfect but people over the centuries have thought that the center, or the heart, was worth transporting. If you can't be in a certain place at a certain time, it is still better to have someone tell you about it than to miss it completely. Asian poetry is too good to miss, and since most English-speaking people will never learn Chinese, Japanese, Korean, Vietnamese or Sanskrit, they will have to read the poems in translation. The sijo poems in this collection were rendered into literal English by a scholar who was born and grew up in Korea. In adapting the poems, I tried to make them more at home in English, adding a word here or there, dropping some, changing some, but always attempting to preserve the way of life which is reflected through these Korean sijo poems. Hopefully, the reader will see in the poetry something of another culture and something of himself or herself, too. As in all poetry worthy of the name, there will be something to learn and something to recognize.

Today, when many Americans are beginning to view their lives as hectic and meaningless, when young and old are escaping to the country to rediscover the purpose and meaning of life, it may be a surprise to find out that fifteenth-century Koreans thought life moved too fast so they retired to the country for mental peace. Man could be what he wanted in a faraway, unknown village isolated from the aggression and worldly affairs of the city where political pressures threatened to corrupt him. The Confucian admired simplicity. For him, "much was much too much." Nature, which was always central to Buddhist thought, was not worshiped but thought of as a partner in life. In nature is found the theme of mutability. All things of this world are merely passing, and so we can accept the falling blossoms, the coming and going of the seasons, the fact of our growing old. We can see ourselves as a small part of the large world.

Some symbols, familiar to the Korean, may not be familiar to the Western reader. Pine, bamboo, chrysanthemum signify courage and loyalty, maintaining an unyielding position in the face of unrighteous circumstances. Peach blossoms remind one of the transient quality of life; plum blossoms are fragile but enduring; a lotus reminds us of the Buddhist concept of purity while stone represents permanence; ravens carry evil omens and egrets symbolize the forces of good. But even without a deep knowledge of the culture, the feelings and the places are there to be experienced and imagined. If flowers look like they are on fire, they are red in all languages. Emotions like love, trust, sorrow, vanity are easily translated, while the values of patriotism and loyalty must be understood within each culture. These sijo poems reflect an age that has disappeared and a way of life that has changed. For us, there is romance in the thought of sitting on straw mats in the light of pine-knot torches. Is that true for a Korean? We, who have never leaned on a jade rail watching a monk disappear into the mist while temple bells echo in the distance, suddenly find ourselves travelers in an exotic world. We turn a page and ponder the way times change and the way they stay the same. What about this?

> To be poor is to be mocked
> To be wealthy is to be hated.

Most sijo poems have more than one level. Some are puzzling and some are crystal clear. When the Buddhist poet wrote:

> The thick dust of this world
> Blinds us to the beauty,

he wasn't thinking of pollution, but what could be more relevant? The "thick dust" of our technologically complex civilization may be blinding us to the beauty of the real world that was there for the Korean poets of the thirteenth, fourteenth and fifteenth centuries, and is still here for us if we look for it.

THE SIJO FORM

The sijo, which is the most popular poetic form in Korean literature, and one of the earliest, is written in three lines. The first line usually states the theme, the second elaborates on it, and the third line is a twist on the theme or a resolution. Sometimes, it is called an anti-theme. A sijo is a more flexible form than a Japanese haiku or tanka poem in that the number of syllables in a sijo varies from forty-one to forty-nine with the average being forty-four syllables. There is no actual punctuation but each line ends with a pause and a caesura, or stop, divides it naturally into two parts. Because the translated lines are awkwardly long in English, the poems are presented here in six lines instead of three. There is no conventional rhyme pattern, but word endings often have similar sounds, and alliteration, assonance, and onomatopoeia are employed frequently.

Originally, sijo poems were written to be sung while the rhythm was beaten on a drum or to lute accompaniment, but today they are written to be read. The sijo poems collected here have been selected from the hundreds that are known and read by Koreans. These are some that have been popular over the centuries and are still loved today.

V. O. B.

For my father, John A. Olsen

Peach and plum blossoms of spring,
Tell me, why are you so proud and vain?
Have you forgotten pine and bamboo,
Green in coldest winter?

Always straight and strong,
They don't come and go with the seasons.

KIM YU-KI

Chrysanthemum, why don't you bloom
When the east winds of March blow?
Only you, chrysanthemum, come into flower
After the leaves have fallen.

You are the only one to count on
In the frosty cold of winter.

YI JUNG-BO

The blue mountains are what they are,
So are the green waters.
The mountains and rivers are what they are.
Why shouldn't I, who live with them, be just what I am?

I want a life as real as theirs
Because I am a part of the universe, too.

KIM IN-HU

Would you like to know who my friends are?
They are water, stone, pine and bamboo.
Oh, and the rising moon from the east mountain
Is a good friend of mine, too.

What more could a person want
Than friends like these eternal five?

YUN SUN-DO

With my harp against my knee,
I drifted off in a pleasant nap.
The dog's bark at the gate wakened me
When my friend came by.

Waiter, bring some rice wine on credit
And, of course, something good to eat, too.

KIM CHANG-UP

The poor old plum tree
Knows that it is spring.
I'm sure she expects
To blossom soon,

But the late spring snowfall
Makes me doubt it.

MAE HWA
(*Plum Blossom*)

Deep in the mountains we have no calendar
To tell us when the seasons change.
Flowers bloom—we guess that it is spring;
Leaves fall, so it is autumn.

And when children hunt for warm clothes,
We know it must be winter!

ANONYMOUS

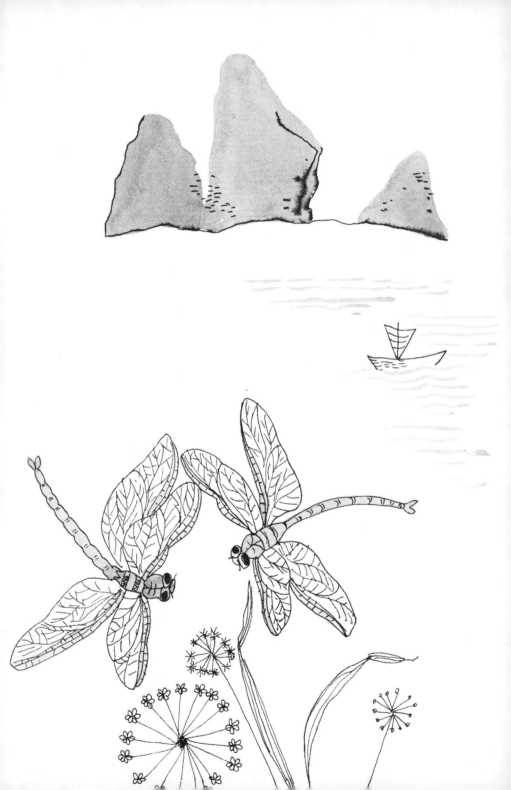

Dragonflies and heron fly together,
Water and sky are the same color blue.
Rowing my little boat
Toward shore, I hear

An old man in a bamboo hat calling across the water.
He is asking for a ride.

KIM CHUN-TAIK

My house is so deep in the woods
That the cuckoo sings in the daytime.
Out here beyond valleys and peaks,
The brushwood gate is pulled shut.

Even the dog, who has forgotten how to bark,
Naps while flowers fall.

ANONYMOUS

In a valley where a stream flows,
I built a cottage on a ledge.
When I plough the soil under the moon
And lie down in the clouds there,

Even the sky and the earth seem to say,
Live and grow old along with us.

ANONYMOUS

What is so amusing about the rain falling
In the clear stream
That red flowers and green trees all over the mountainside
Are bursting into waves of laughter?

Oh well, let them laugh as long as they like
For they have only a few days to enjoy the spring wind.

KING HYO-JONG

Birds, do not blame the blossoms
For falling;
It is not their fault
That the wind scatters them.

And what is the good of chiding spring
Just as she is leaving?

SONG SOON

Standing here with my hand on the jade rail
And my lute on my back,
All I see through the drizzling rain
Are peach blossoms falling in the east wind,

While sad birds sing
Farewell to spring.

ANONYMOUS

Butterfly, let's fly to the green mountains!
You, too, tiger swallowtail!
When it grows dark, we can
Curl up in a flower.

If the flower isn't friendly,
We'll sleep on a leaf instead.

ANONYMOUS

Butterflies playing happily
In a hundred-flowered garden,
Beware. Though each fragrance lures you,
Try not to light on every flower.

Sunset may find you
Entangled in a spider web.

ANONYMOUS

Only white gull and I
Know about the thirty-six peaks of Mount Chung-Ryang.
White gull will never tell anyone
But I am suspicious of you, peach blossom.

You might fall into the stream
And, floating by, tell the fishermen about our secret place.

YI HWANG

I close my book and open the window:
There is a boat floating on the lake.
Gulls, what are you thinking,
As you fly back and forth over the water?

If only you knew how tempted I am
To drop my dreams and follow you, my friends.

CHUNG ON

A flock of sparrows, chattering
In the after sunset dusk.
Half a branch would do
For birds as small as you.

What is the good of squabbling
Over such a big bush?

ANONYMOUS

Wind last night blew down
A gardenful of peach blossoms.
A boy with a broom
Is starting to sweep them up.

Fallen flowers are flowers still;
Don't brush them away.

ANONYMOUS

When a shadow appeared on the water,
I looked up to see a monk crossing the bridge.
Stay, I said, so I could ask
Where he was going.

But, pointing at white clouds, he moved on,
Answering without words.

ANONYMOUS

In a hermit's cottage, silent, still,
I sit all alone with nobody.
A white cloud dozes
To the strains of a quiet song.

No one can know
How happy I am!

KIM SOO-JANG

On these summer days,
I have nothing to do.
Were it not for the afternoon crowing of cocks
In a deep bush of bamboo,

Nothing would waken me
From an empty dream in a deep sleep.

SUNG HON

Only half-awakened from a nap on my pine-needle bed,
I open my sleepy eyes
To discover seagulls swooping in and out
Over the sunset-colored harbor.

I wonder, am I the only one
To know this sweet moment?

KIM SAM-HYUN

Rain is falling on the paulownia
And the sound of each drop on each leaf
Is sorrowful to me
For today I am filled with sadness.

I'll never plant
A broad-leafed tree again.

KIM SANG-YONG

It rained
And now the pomegranate is in bloom.
I look out across the lotus pond
From beneath the rolled-up crystal-beaded blind.

I wish I could tell someone
How sad I am.

SHIN HEUM

The temple cannot be far
Since I hear the sound of drumbeats.
It is high on the mountaintop
Under white clouds, they told me.

But how will I ever find it
With all these clouds floating around me?

ANONYMOUS

Don't bring out the straw mat;
I'll sit on fallen leaves.
Don't bother to light the pine-knot torch;
The moon will rise again tonight.

But I might say yes to wine
And a little dish of mountain herbs.

HAN HWAK

When darkness covers the mountain village,
A dog, far away, begins to bark.
Opening the brushwood door, I find
The night is cold and the moon is bright.

Why do you think that dog is barking
At the sleepy moon over the mountain?

CHUN KEUM

Why should you envy the fish
Who plays in the water?
No sooner does the fisherman leave
Than an egret swoops down in search of him.

Up and down, in and around, all day long—
A fish's life is a hard life.

YI JUNG-BO

Hey there, white seagull!
What are you doing?
Is it a fish you are seeking
Deep in those reeds?

Why work so hard?
Come fall asleep like lazy me.

KIM KWANG-WUK

Is that a cuckoo singing?
Are the willows growing green?
Smoke is rising from the cottages
Of the fishing village at suppertime.

I think the season has begun!
Bring out the old fishing net, my boy.

YUN SUN-DO

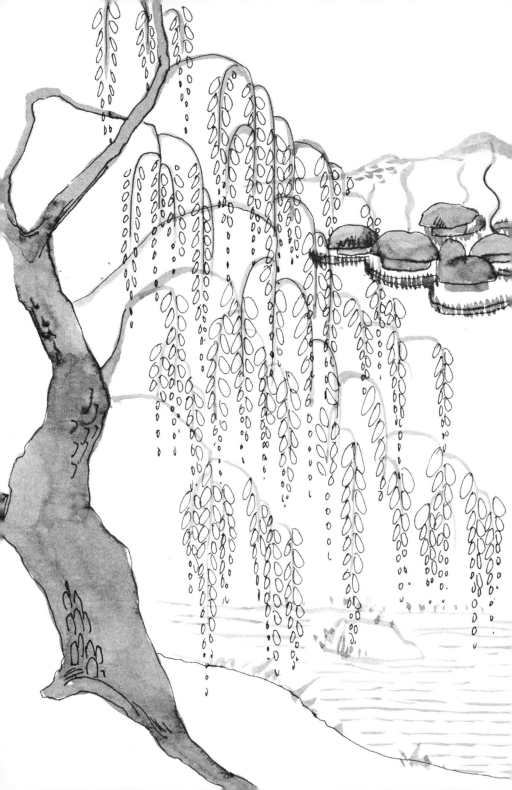

The river darkens on an autumn night
And the waves subside as if to sleep.
I drop a line into the water
But the sleepy fish won't bite.

The empty boat and I return
Filled with our catch of moonlight.

YI JUNG

A fisherman discouraged by a storm,
Sold his boat and bought a horse;
But dragging a load up winding mountain paths
Is no better.

Now he thinks he will not work on a boat,
Or on a horse, but on a farm instead.

CHANG MANN

Ten years it took
To build my little cottage.
Now the cool wind inhabits half of it
And the rest is filled with moonlight.

There is no place left for the mountain and the stream
So I guess they will have to stay outside.

SONG SOON

Though there is still quite a way to go,
Home is only across that ridge.
The moon is already rising
Over the narrow lane cut between pines.

But how can I hurry my donkey on,
When he is hungry today, as every day.

ANONYMOUS

Blessed is today;
Today is a happy day.
There is no other day like today,
Not yesterday, not tomorrow.

If every day were like today,
What in the world would I worry about?

KIM KOO

What if a rafter is too short or too long?
What if a beam is aslant or askew?
This thatch-roofed cottage is mine;
Do not laugh because it is so small.

All that moonlight is mine, too,
Spread out over the grassy hill.

SHIN HEUM

On the small table, the early mellowed
Red ripe persimmons are a lovely sight.
They may not be so rare as citrons,
Still I would like to hide one in my pocket.

But, oh, since my parents are gone,
There is nobody to surprise with pretty things.

PARK IN-RO

The Great Bear has moved across the sky
But the moon is still visible.
I cannot tell how far we've rowed
But I know the night is fading now.

The wind whispers of women beating clothes;
I guess we must be almost there.

YI JUNG-JIN

What is love like?
Is it round or is it square?
Long or short? Is there more
To measure than what I'm stepping on?

You may not think it lasts long
But I can't see where it ends.

ANONYMOUS

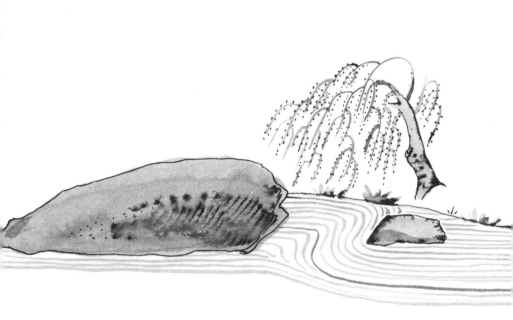

Even the thousand-sprayed green willow
Can't hold spring wind when it must go;
Bees and butterflies must watch helplessly
When summer flowers fade.

So it is now with my love leaving,
And we are close as wind and willow.

YI WUN-ICK

Oh, do not pull yourself away
If I, weeping, grasp your sleeve.
You have a long way to go over the hills,
And it is almost dark.

In the lonely night ahead, you will understand,
When you must light the lamp alone.

YI MYUNG-HAN

These few shoots cut from a mountain willow,
I send to you, my love.
Plant them under your window,
Watch over them,

And when night rain falls on tender leaves,
Think of me.

HONG NANG

I'd like to carve a moon
Out of my heart
And hang it ninety thousand miles
High in the sky

So it would shine on the place
Where my love is tonight.

CHUNG CHUL

When I think about why
You sent that fan to me,
I wonder if you meant
For me to blow out the fire in my heart.

How could I put out a fire with a fan
When teardrops failed?

ANONYMOUS

On the hill in spring
All the half-bloomed flowers are on fire.
There is rain
To drown that fire

But there is a fire inside of me
And even an ocean couldn't put it out.

KIM DUK-RYUNG

A frosty dawn, a waning moon,
The cry of a lonely goose,
And hope is born again
Of hearing news from you.

But only an empty sound drifts
From distant bluish clouds.

ANONYMOUS

My love is a thousand miles away
And the sorrow of parting
Lies too deep,
So I came to the river

Where the water can soothe my mind
And weep sadness away in the night.

WANG BANG-YUN

If teardrops were pearls,
I would catch them as they fell.
Ten years from now, when my love returns,
We could live in a castle of pearl!

What a shame that tears are lost
As soon as they drop.

ANONYMOUS

A mountain
Stays always blue,
A river
Flows on, day and night.

Would that we human beings
Might flourish forever like mountain and river!

YI HWANG

Long and lonely December night,
I wish I could cut you in two,
And keep one half under my covers,
Warm and sweetly scented,

So I might add it to a shorter night
When my love sleeps here with me.

HWANG CHINI

Mount Taishan is high and steep
But it is only a mountain under the sky.
If you tried, slowly and surely,
You could climb to the top.

But before you even try, you are ready to give up,
Saying it is too high.

SA EUN YANG

If everyone were a chief,
Who would be a farmer?
If the doctor could cure every disease,
Would there be so many graves in Mt. Pukmang?

Bring me another bowl of wine,
I'll do what I please all day long.

KIM CHANG-UP

Do not blow in the garden, wind!
Over the snow and under the moon.
I am almost sure that the sounds I hear
Are not the footsteps of sandaled feet.

But because I am lonely,
I keep hoping to hear my love returning.
                                    ANONYMOUS

How I'd like to live
Under a peaceful sky in a peaceful world,
With a gourd on my back and my sleeves hanging loose,
Swinging in the wind.

Why wish for a dream?
Whatever the world says, I'm free.
                                    YANG UNG-JEUNG

If you talk too much, you are a swindler.
If you talk too little, a fool.
To be poor is to be mocked,
To be wealthy is to be hated.

I think that to live under this sky
Is a difficult thing.

KIM SANG-YONG

Do not delight in what you own,
Do not desire what you haven't.
Those who do not have, do not know
What a worry it is for those who have.

Such a pity to see so many people
Scrambling for things.

YI JUNG-BO

At the first sign of my horse's fright,
I tightened the reins and looked down.
Green mountains in silken splendor
Stood submerged in water.

Poor horse, do not be frightened,
I only came to look.

ANONYMOUS

Since wild geese flew south,
Many frosty mornings have passed
And the fall nights have lengthened,
Deepening the traveler's yearning.

Only a midnight gardenful of moonlight
Can make him feel at home.

JO MYUNG-RI

North wind blows hard through the trees
And the white moon shines coldly on the snow.
At this frontier castle far from home,
I stand watch with my sword drawn,

Ready to make the world tremble at my command.
What stands in my way?

KIM JONG-SU

In this faraway village where the snow has melted,
Dark clouds hover overhead.
Where are the early plum blossoms
That should be blooming now?

Standing alone in the sunset,
I think that I have lost my way.

                                        YI SEK

"Pine tree in the green mountain,
Why do you lie on the cold ground?"
"I could not stop the cold and frost,
So my roots came up, and I fell down.

If you meet a master artisan on your way,
Tell him, please, that I will be waiting here."

                                        ANONYMOUS

I left home without my umbrella
For the north sky was clear.
Now it is snowing in the mountains
And raining in the fields.

After walking in the cold rain,
I hope I will find a warm bed to sleep in!

KIM JAE

While your parents are here,
Love them and do your best.
After they are gone, there's no use crying
Over undone acts of love.

There are things
You can't make up for.

CHUNG CHUL

I have lived up half my life already
And I know I can't be young again
But I'd like to stop right here
And not grow any older.

Try, white hair, to understand.
Slow down your pace, at least.

YI MYUNG-HAN

My ancestors can't see me
And I can't see them;
Although I do not see them,
I can see the path they trod.

If I see the path, is there
A reason not to follow it?

YI HWANG

Am I really old, as people say?
I wonder if old people feel this way.
I am happy in a field of flowers;
It only takes a cup of wine to cheer me.

But I cannot keep gusts of autumn wind
From blowing through my white hair.

KIM JUNG-KU

Let me ask you, Mind,
What is the secret of your eternal youth?
My body is old
But you have no trouble keeping up with it.

If I acted as young as I feel,
I'm afraid everyone would laugh at me.

ANONYMOUS

I hold a rod in one hand,
Grasp a thorn in the other.
Let the thorn bar the path to growing old,
Let the rod keep away white hair.

But alas, white hair comes anyway,
Taking another road.

WOO TAHK

Old man weighed down with a bundle on your head
And a bundle on your back,
Let me carry all that for you.
I am young; even a boulder is not too heavy for me.

To be old is sad enough
Without making life harder.

CHUNG CHUL

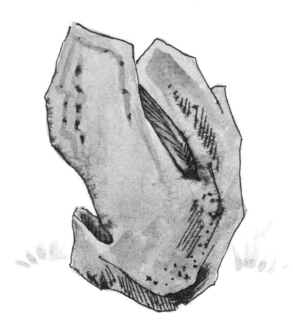

What shall I be
When I am dead?
I will be the oldest and tallest pine tree
On the highest peak of Bong Nae,

And when white snow covers all the world,
I will still be green.

SUNG SAM MUN

I like you, bamboo,
You are a true friend.
When I was young,
I played on stilts with you;

Now that I am old, you stand outside my window
Waiting till I need a walking stick.

KIM KWANG-WUK

Look below you. The river is a thousand fathoms deep.
Look behind you. Deep mountains far as you can see.
The thick dust of this world
Blinds us to the beauty,

But when the moon lights the night,
It is easier to forget the world's troubles.

YI HYUN-BO

You, blue stream, flowing around mountains,
Do not be proud of moving so swiftly.
Once you get to the open sea,
You will never be able to return.

Why not stop for a moment while the bright moon
Gleams down on the world?

HWANG CHINI

About the Editor

VIRGINIA OLSEN BARON is the editor of *The Seasons of Time*, a collection of Japanese tanka poetry, and *Here I Am*, an anthology of poetry written by young people of America's minority groups.

About the Artist

MINJA PARK KIM was born in Korea and educated at Seoul National University, from which she graduated with honors in the field of fine arts. She is a gifted painter and textile designer, as well as the illustrator of two previous children's books. Ms. Kim lives with her husband and two daughters in Sunnyside, New York.

About the Book

This book was set in Linotype Janson and printed by offset lithography, with photo display in Time Script Semibold and News Gothic Condensed. The artist used pen, brush and ink with wash in preparing the illustrations.